AND GOD CREATED HUMMUS

poems by
David Silverman

GLASS LYRE PRESS

Copyright © 2019 David Silverman
Paperback ISBN: 978-1-941783-65-8

All rights reserved: Except for the purpose of quoting brief passages for review, no part of this book may be reproduced or transmitted in any form or by any means, electronic or mechanical, including photocopying, recording, or by any information storage and retrieval system, without permission in writing from the publisher.

Design & Layout: Steven Asmussen
Cover Art: Rebecca Silverman
Copyediting: Linda E. Kim

Glass Lyre Press, LLC
P.O. Box 2693
Glenview, IL 60025
www.GlassLyrePress.com

And God Created Hummus

dedicated to
LVNELVN

Tell me you don't matter to a universe that conspired
To give you such a tongue
Such rhythm or rhythmless hips,
Such opposable thumbs.
Give thanks or go home, a waste of spark.
Speak or let the maker take back your throat.
March or let the creator rescind your feet.
Dream or let your god destroy your good and fertile mind.
This is your warning.
This is your birthright.
Do not let this universe regret you!

—Marty McConnell

What is this world, but the body of God?

—Barbara Crooker

What will survive of us is love.

—Philip Larkin

Contents

And God Created Hummus	1
Parting with My Prayer Shawl, Made By My Daughter, Upon the Zombie Apocalypse	4
Mileage Plus	5
Seeking Something	6
Of No Help Whatsoever to My Wife, Organizing Our Bookshelves	7
Today	8
To My Wife	9
34B, a Middle Seat, On the Red-Eye	10
How Cupid Saved My Marriage	11
At the Writers' Workshop, I Am Instructed to "Write Dirty"	12
Upon Listening to Muzak in My Cardiologist's Waiting Room	13
Some Things, You Just Have to Learn for Yourself	14
A Simple Prayer	15
The Significance of the Insignificant	16
Love is Stronger Than Death	17
Holy, Holy, Holy	18
There Have Been Times, Love	19
Write, Pray, Love	20
Because We Are in Love	21
11:11. That is All.	22
Anniversary Poem	23
Why I Write Poetry	24
On My 50th Birthday, I Channel Ogden Nash	25
Random Walk	26
Mind Over Matter	27
Mindfulness	28
Foreign Exchange: Jerusalem '79	29

On the 150th Anniversary of the Publication, in Warsaw, of My Great-Grandfather's 13-Volume Edition of the Bible	30
What We Needed	31
How I Came to Compare Visiting My Sick Uncle to Taking Fish Oil Pills	32
Having Never Written a Holocaust Poem, I Write This	33
To Be a Jew in the Twenty-First Century	34
On the Jewish New Year	35
In the Age of Giants	36
A Man Shall Not Lie	37
Fathers and Sons	38
On the Day His Father Died, Esau Wept	39
Dinah Took a Walk One Lovely Day	40
The Four Species	41
Because	42
Upon Unexpectedly Finding a Long-Forgotten Keepsake	43
Advice to My Children About Handling Criticism	44
Upon Seeing My Children's Newly Built School for the First Time	45
How Deeply Rooted is the Tree of Life	46
My Son-in-Law, the Rabbi, is a Clown	47
Upon Meeting my Granddaughter for the First Time	48
What Jessica Hears	49
Matt Turns Six	50
What Matters	51
The Pain That Cuts Deep	52
A Soldier Learns to Sleep	54
A Little Bit Good, A Little Bit Not So Good	55

Leaving Home	56
"My Name Is Rebecca...But Most People Call Me Reby"	58
Watching a Football Game Before Dawn With My 10-Year-Old Son	59
Shooting Hoops Before Dawn With My 16-Year-Old Son	60
Upon Speaking to My Son's High School Basketball Team Before What Turns Out to be Their Final Game	61
Ode to Our High School Gym	63
Boys Fool Themselves That They Can Fly	64
Trader's Lament	65
As All Martyrs, Should Be Remembered	66
Miracles	67
Acknowledgements	69

And God Created Hummus

In preparation for a talk I was to give in my synagogue
on the first section of Genesis—the one in which God
creates the world in 6 days, including Adam and Eve,
and rests on the seventh—I printed out a scholarly essay
entitled, And God Created Humans.

My printer, however, is very old and with every exertion,
wheezes like a coal miner might after 40 years in the mine,
which seems like something I could say about myself, climbing
a staircase or running to catch a bus, though I can't remember
the last time I took a bus. But I'm straying from the point,

which is the ink did not transfer smoothly to the paper
and the resulting smear and shadow obscured some of
the words, such that it appeared the title of the essay
was no longer, And God Created Humans.
Rather, it read, And God Created Hummus.

I stopped, for a moment, to consider what an article entitled,
And God Created Hummus, might describe. On which day
would God have created the hummus? It wouldn't be the first day,
because even the most skillful hummus-maker would need some
light to find a bowl and utensils with which to grind the chickpeas.

And, of course, God hadn't, yet, created chickpeas.
It also seems God wouldn't have bothered to create hummus
on the days he created the animals and fish, because without
opposable thumbs and submerged beneath the seas, these
creatures could never hope to enjoy the pleasure of pushing

a pita shovel through a plate of creamy hummus. No, God
must have created hummus on the day he created humans.
And it occurred to me, maybe the Tree of Knowledge wasn't
an apple tree but a chickpea tree! Though I know chickpeas
don't grow on trees, perhaps in the Garden of Eden they did;

the hardy, beige globes, hanging low and irresistible, waiting
to be picked and soaked and mashed and stirred, then spread
on a plate, a puddle of olive oil pooled in the center, warm and
virginal—the most virginal oil ever pressed—and, then, some fat
fava beans, soaking like old Jews in a hot tub in Boca Raton.

But unlike old Jews, fava beans are delicious. And, yet again,
my mind's meandered from the hummus creation story. So,
I type the words "And God Created Hummus," into my browser
and, after taking a quick peek at a site called *HummusXXX*
(which I immediately delete from my browser history),

I'm directed to a website which gives the top 10 reasons
to eat hummus, including: "Because Natalie Portman and
Al Gore are totally obsessed with hummus." This hardly
seems a reason that *I* should eat hummus, but it turns out
they are both vegans. Just like Adam and Eve!

And, now, I think of Nat and Al, naked in Eden, sharing a plate of
hummus and moaning with pleasure. Al is a sloppy eater—she will
come to hate that about him in the hundreds of years ahead—but,
tonight, when a bit of hummus sticks to the side of his cheek, she
kisses it away. And though God has created Natalie Portman from

Al Gore's rib and though they are to be fruitful and multiply, I am
disgusted. He is old enough to be her father, for God's sake. But
before I banish the image of the two hummus-obsessed lovers,
my mind drifts to a scene in black and white. Both Nat and Al are
dressed in trench coats and stylish hats and Claude Rains ushers

Victor Laszlo onto a plane out of Casablanca (a place you can
probably find some fine hummus). And, before they part, Natalie,
with tears in her eyes, says "But, Al, what about us?" to which
the former vice president and inventor of the Internet, replies,
"We'll always have hummus. Here's looking at you kid."

And I know this is silly. And I know this is just my way of putting
off writing the talk that everyone expects; in which I will present
the same themes as a thousand speakers before me. So, I want
nothing more than to stand in front of them and talk about hummus.
Not the dubious top 10 reasons they should eat hummus,

but about that day in Jerusalem, I took you to Pinat Hahummus
for the first time. I want to tell them how the waiter glared at us
when we asked for a menu. I want to tell them how the pita was
so hot it burnt my fingers when I split it open. I want to tell them
how the oil and beans slid down my throat, like an elixir that ought

to be bottled and sold at county fairs, to cure what ails you.
I want to tell them how beautiful the simplest things can be.
How the world was created in six days. How much Adam loved Eve.
And how much I loved you when, sloppy eater that I am, you moved
next to me and kissed away a stray bit of hummus from my cheek.

Parting with My Prayer Shawl, Made By My Daughter, Upon the Zombie Apocalypse

My wife and I are talking with our friend Molly, in synagogue,
just before services begin. Molly compliments the prayer shawl
draped over my shoulders, whose colorful collar has stitched into it,
an elaborate needlepoint depicting the Old City of Jerusalem.
I tell her that my daughter made the collar for me and add,
if our house caught fire and I could run in and save only one thing,
it would be the shawl. Realizing, an instant too late, that I've prioritized
an inanimate object over my wife of 36 years, Lauren shoots me
an incredulous look and says, "Seriously? I'm standing right here."

Thankfully, I see she is more amused than annoyed and, contrary
to my faux pas, I have often insisted that (a) I would surely run into
a burning building to save her; (b) I would donate a kidney to her,
if she needed one; and (c) if she committed a crime and was sent
to jail, I would wait for her, no matter how long she is gone.
And even though she has informed me that if *I* am sent to jail,
she will not reciprocate my grand gesture, it changes nothing.
This woman, who has taken care of me in a thousand ways,
who has given me children, who accepts me notwithstanding
my general cluelessness and frequent gaffes, has earned my fealty.

So, the bullet meant for Lauren will have to pass through me first,
and any internal organ she wants, is hers for the asking. And, when
the zombie apocalypse begins, she knows I will sacrifice myself
and tell her to run. After we embrace, for what may be the last time,
I'll wrap her in the prayer shawl made by our daughter, the vibrant
blues and reds and yellows providing some cheer in a bleak world
overrun by the living dead. And, before she leaves, I tell her what
she already knows: that if, somehow, the zombies are vanquished,
she can return the shawl to me at home, where I will be waiting.
No matter how long she is gone.

Mileage Plus

Too often, I travel alone. Hating airports. Hating hotels.
Hating anywhere that isn't home. But I look forward
to unpacking my bag; to finding the cards you've hidden,
inside a jacket or beneath some rolled-up socks, one for
each day we'll be apart. Sometimes Hallmark's best—
$5.99 for Alvin and the Chipmunks singing the first
two lines of *Leavin' on a Jet Plane*—but more often,
a generic greeting from the 99-cent section. And on the
inside of each card, your own handwritten messages:
loving affirmations, the occasional suggestive drawing,
and private jokes, incomprehensible to anyone who isn't us.
These cards are more important to me than toothpaste,
more important than my lucky business-meeting underwear
(Yes, I have lucky underwear). Once, away for two weeks,
lonely and jetlagged, I opened all fourteen envelopes
when I got to my Hong Kong hotel. Terrible, I know.
Made worse when, intuiting my transgression, you accused me
of inappropriate card-recipient behavior, which I insisted
was not actually a thing and which I categorically denied.
I'm sorry for allowing you to apologize. That was wrong.
Especially, the second time.

Do you know, I've kept your cards in a big box in the basement,
mixed among old tax returns and expired appliance warranties?
So many cards, I can't remember them all. But, one time, we were
arguing about some long-forgotten matter just before a trip, when
my taxi arrived to take me away. Hours later, when I got to my hotel,
still angry at you, I opened my bag and found the card—the perfect card
I did not deserve—that you somehow managed to slip in when I wasn't looking.
On the outside flap was a picture of a voodoo doll stabbed from head to toe,
beneath which it said: "Thinking of You."

And inside, you wrote, "I love you, you know. The rest is commentary."

Seeking Something

We are always seeking, seeking something. Love. Place. Security. Enlightenment. Acceptance. Peace. This is not about God (though it may be about God). But it is definitely about faith. It is definitely about purpose. We seek something to believe in. Something that matters. Something about which we can say, *I belong to this. This is mine.* This Something seems close, like a song you've heard a thousand times, whose words you can't recall; like a dream interrupted by the insensitive beep, beep, beep of your alarm clock. You think of Mrs. Winfield, your sixth-grade home-room teacher. Once, arriving early to class, you spied her spraying perfume on her left wrist, saw her raise that wrist to inhale the fragrance, then rub her wrists together. You look away. You know you have seen something you had no right to see. But you have seen it and you find excuses to approach her desk over and over that day and for the rest of the year. What is it you want? She is a married woman. You are a kid who collects baseball cards. You do not know what perfume she wore. But, whenever you smell that scent, in a crowded elevator or on the street, it takes you back to her desk. And tonight, you watch your wife of thirty years dress. She does not know you are watching or, perhaps, she does. And when she takes a small bottle from the counter, sprays her left wrist, raises it to her face to inhale the fragrance and, then, rubs her wrists together, you think—*I belong to this. This is mine. This is really something.*

Of No Help Whatsoever to My Wife, Organizing Our Bookshelves

Lauren is organizing our bookshelves, truly troubled that,
over time, books have migrated from the original spots
carefully chosen for them. Novels among non-fiction,
mysteries mixed with memoirs, self-help hobnobbing
with history and, even, some poetry and humor books
standing side-by-side, as if to proclaim they belong together!

The symbolism is lost on my wife, a professional organizer,
who cherishes order. As if neatness can, somehow, soften
the jagged edges of the world. She spies a volume by Amichai,
sandwiched between a book of essays by David Sedaris and one
by Calvin Trillin and returns the epic poet to his rightful spot
between Akhmatova and Ashbery, excellent company both.

Not caring, whatsoever, which books go where, and feeling the need
to make a larger point, I mention that, "Some poems are funny.
Some of my poems, for instance." Lauren looks at me, organizing
her thoughts—keeping my fragile ego in order is a job for a professional.
But, finally (and failing to suppress a smile), she grants me this:

"Yes, you are a funny, funny man."

I wonder what she means by the second "funny."
But, sometimes, you just need to know how to take a compliment.

Today

Today, I secretly watched you eat breakfast.
A bit of oatmeal clung to the corner of your mouth.
I probably shouldn't have let you leave the house like that.

Today, I promised to do something you asked me to do,
but can't recall what it was. I hope it doesn't involve
picking you up at a certain time or refrigerating perishable items.

Today, I thought of your body as an object.
Which is wrong, I know. But had you seen yourself
exit the room in those skinny jeans, you might understand.

Today, I conjured a moment when we were young.
Not a specific moment, but an amalgam of all the moments.
A bottomless bowl of moments.

Today, you smiled at me, for no particular reason,
and I thought: that should be an app.

To My Wife

> ...for your face, I have exchanged all faces
> —*Philip Larkin, To My Wife*

I did not choose you because you are beautiful,
though you are beautiful.

And I did not choose you because you are wise,
wiser than I am in all that matters.

I did not choose you because you chose me, instead of him
(thank you, by the way, for that).

And I did not choose you because you loved me,
when no one should have.

I chose you because I had no choice in the matter,
the moment I saw your face.

34B, a Middle Seat, On the Red-Eye

To my left is a tattooed man, including one on his neck that says Stella.
It's rude, probably unwise, but I can't help staring. Is Stella his wife?
His mother? A bar girl he met in Bangkok, who killed herself when
she found out he would not keep his promise to bring her Stateside?
Or, is he part of some well-read street gang that reveres the work of
Tennessee Williams? To my right, is a pretty woman of, as they say,
a "certain age," who went a little overboard with the Botox.
Why do women do this? Like tattoos, every wrinkle tells a story.
She, too, is fascinated with 34A's neck, sees me seeing her, smiles at me
(as much as she possibly can). The mind wanders. How cool would it be
if her name is Stella? Away too long, I miss you, my own Stella.
The wrinkles on your neck, by your eyes. The most interesting story I know.

How Cupid Saved My Marriage

When you were born, I was two months and twenty-three days old.
And on that day, the Committee on Prospective Matches convened
a meeting in celestial chambers, to discuss the matter of us.

Cupid looked around the table at the assembled angels and felt
a headache coming on. He wanted to get home for dinner,
but knew this would not be easy.

They all spoke at once:

He'll be a slob!
He won't listen!
He'll forget her birthday!
He'll snore!

She deserves better, said a prissy angel, whom Cupid had never liked.
Just look at her (a Power Point slide of a beautiful baby girl was projected
across a nearby cloud. The angels sighed in admiration). The priss checked
her notes: *I have a nice boy born just last week. He's going to be a doctor!*

They babbled on and Cupid massaged his temples, no longer listening.
If this kept up, he would never get home and she was serving pot roast tonight,
his favorite.

These angels were always so sure of the math, but the calculus of couples
defies the rational laws of nature. Though he had to admit, the match looked
bad on the surface, there was something about the combination of these two
that made him smile. In the end, it was his call and he declared, *Enough!*
They're right for each other, I'm going home.

But, Cupid, the priss cried: *what about the snoring?*

They'll work it out, he said, thinking of his own deviated septum.

He could not wait to get home to tell his wife about his day.

At the Writers' Workshop, I Am Instructed to "Write Dirty"

You get me hot baby. Really, really hot.
So hot, *you give me fever,* as the song says,
at least 98.8 and I want a popsicle so much,
I'd sell state secrets to get one (if I knew any).
But one popsicle won't be enough.
I need an ice cream truck, a fleet of them.
I need to age for a few weeks in a walk-in freezer,
like a piece of meat. To be flash frozen
in a freak alpine storm for a thousand years,
just to stop sweating. Or better yet, insert me
(oh baby, insert me), into a subliminal ad,
among the ice cubes in a tumbler of scotch,
making love on some exotic beach.
Drunk, as always, with the pleasure of you.

Upon Listening to Muzak in My Cardiologist's Waiting Room

> All of me, why not take all of me?
> —*Frank Sinatra*

To give you my heart, love, seems terribly trite,
but what if I told you, you could have my liver?
My lungs? My islets of Langerhans? What if
I said you could have it all? Kneecaps? Yours!
Epidermis? Yours! Every muscle, every nerve,
every bony protrusion. Yours! Yours! Yours!
If you said you wanted my fingernails, I'd pull
them out one by one and make a necklace you
could wear to parties. And though I might feel
like staying home—missing vital organs, fingers
bleeding—I will be there by your side, so that
everyone knows I belong to you.

Some Things, You Just Have to Learn for Yourself

Cancer gets a kick out of pulling the covers off late at night.
Cancer has a bad attitude and doesn't play well with others.
Cancer is a sliver of glass that disappears into the fleshy part of your foot.
Cancer is burnt toast, moldy fruit, the wine that's turned.
Cancer is the job that should have been yours but went to that idiot in Sales.
Cancer is the Reply All you wish you could get back and will have to answer for.
Cancer is a wet knot in your shoelace, a size 17 neck in a size 16 shirt.
Cancer is termites in the wall, a gestating rat in the attic.
Cancer is a dead battery on the coldest day of the year.
Cancer is an airball, a fourth quarter fumble, a called third strike
with the bases full.
Cancer is a migratory bird, minding its own business, sucked into the engine
of a jumbo jet.
Cancer is the unexpected thunderclap overhead and the storm you thought
was miles away, is here.

A Simple Prayer

Blessed are the caregivers, who try to shield me
from infection and fear. Their kindness washes
over me and irrigates my thirsty soul. Let me get
well quickly, so the recipient can become the giver.

Blessed are the surgeons, who remove what does
not belong in my body. Give them the vision to see
more than the lines drawn across my torso and around
my wounded breast. Help them see that I am not a
procedure, but a mother, wife, daughter, sister, friend.

Blessed are the nurses, who engage me in conversation
and adjust my pillows; who look with disapproval when
I say, I'm not hungry. May the hospital give them healthy
raises, award stock options, declare a day in their honor
(On Nurse's Day, all bedpans will be emptied by doctors).

Blessed are the visitors, who fidget in uncomfortable chairs.
Who exchange the fresh oxygen in their lungs, for the stale air
of my hospital room. Remember their selfless offering
and, at the end, grant them one deep, final, sweet breath,
to enjoy forever, in the world-to-come.

Blessed is my body, created in Your image.
Heal my scars: the ones that can be seen in a mirror
and those that can only be seen when the lights are out.

This is my simple prayer.

May it be acceptable.

Blessed is God, let Him say, *ENOUGH!*

I sing a happy song.

The Significance of the Insignificant

> This was a day when nothing happened...
> a day that unwrapped itself like an unexpected gift.
> —Barbara Crooker, *Ordinary Life*

Bread and butter. Long, hot showers. Taking a nap. Waking
from a nap. Getting a laugh from one of my kids. My T-shirt,
drenched after a workout. The way a basketball feels as it
leaves my fingertips. Writing the first, the fifth, the tenth draft
of a poem I may never finish. And, even, the plastic bracelet
snapped around my wrist. The sharp sting of the IV needle.
The cold air on my backside, as I shuffle down a hospital hall.
Nothing is simple. Everything is simple. Nothing is simple.
A butterfly flaps its wings in China and I eat a bag of M & Ms.
But light is sweet, and it feels good to turn my face to the sun.
And, of course, there's your fragrant neck, your beating heart.
These I appreciate most of all. There will never be another me.
There will never be another you. And, though there may be
a billion galaxies, each containing a billion planets, there will
never be another day exactly like this. An insignificant day.
When I followed you upstairs and you unwrapped yourself
for me, like an unexpected gift.

Love is Stronger Than Death

> For the sake of my love, place me as a seal upon your heart...
> because love is stronger than death...
> —*Song of Songs 8:6*

I want to believe my love will protect you after I am gone.
That it will fill the cracks in the windowsills to keep you warm
and bolt the door shut every night before you go to sleep.

Which is funny, in a way, because I'm too lazy to caulk those windows
and often forget to check the door before we go to sleep.

But when you are cold, you place your body next to mine and steal my warmth.

And, if anyone breaks in, you know I will sacrifice myself and tell you to run,
which, of course, you will not do (God forbid, I tell you anything).

So, I will believe this: love is stronger than the cold night air
and love is stronger than a midnight intruder.

As for love and death, I am content to wait a while to find out.
With you. In our drafty, open-doored home.

Holy, Holy, Holy

> Behold the bush burned with fire and the bush was not consumed...
> Take your shoes from your feet, for the place you are standing upon,
> is holy ground.
>
> —*Exodus 3:2-5*

Our house is no work of art. Nothing any passing driver
would slow down to ogle. But the walls are plumb,
the floorboards quiet. It's a good house in which to eat a meal.
To watch a ball game or write a poem. To have an argument.
To make love. It's a good house, in which to heal.

Here, we were tested in a thousand ways.
Here, we raised our children.
Here, faith and fidelity reign.

We praise the pear tree in the front yard. The pine trees
in the back. The flower beds that bloom each spring.

Once, the backyard grill got too hot and, when I opened the hood
flames singed my face. "Poof, no eyebrows," you joked.

That night, I dreamed the house caught fire, yet, it was not consumed.
And in my dream, the flowers stood and swayed, the pear tree bowed,
the pine trees chanted as one: *"Holy. Holy. Holy."*

And I removed the shoes from my feet and called your name.

There Have Been Times, Love

There have been times, love, when, if you were not
the magnanimous person you are, you would have
wished me dead. Or mute (for a while, at least).

Long enough to count to ten or, even, ten-thousand,
depending on my transgression. Long enough to get your nails done.
Long enough for me to appreciate what a jackass I can be.

If only there were a remote control, with which you could rewind
to the opening credits or fast forward to the happy ending.
Or even, when necessary, shut me off entirely.

You wonder how a man so considerate of others, can be so
insensitive when it comes to you, of all people: the one who,
at bedtime, will decide where a sleeping dog will lie.

I will say this (though it pains me to admit): while you are not always right,
your track record is far better than mine. It would be logical, then,
to simply give in the next time, the time after that, and so on and so on,

until I've forgotten how to raise my voice in anger.
Until I am accepting as a leaf, swaying in whatever direction the wind blows.
But you are far too clever to be taken in by such pretense and, anyhow,

what you've always wanted me to understand, is that winning
has never been the point. Magnanimous you. Insensitive me.
Don't you know, love? I have always understood.

We fight, to protect that which we cherish.

Write, Pray, Love

> In certain ways, writing is a form of prayer.
> —Denise Levertov

The sages teach that a Jew should recite 100 blessings every day.
Assuming 8 hours sleep, this requires a blessing every 9.6 minutes,

on average. And though I only sleep 5 hours a night, giving me 1.8
minutes more, on average, over the well-rested Jew, this is too much

for me. But I do pray, in my own way, eschewing the traditional words
written by rabbis (who thought so little of women, that they thanked God

for not making them one). Instead, I think of the poets I admire:
Jews and gentiles, men and women, believers and non, sinners all.

While those around me sway and chant "The 18 Blessings," I close my
eyes and think of sad Anne Sexton, who killed herself, but left us this:

"There is joy in all; in the hair I brush each morning, in the Cannon towel, newly washed...in the chapel of eggs I cook each morning...All this is God."

And Mary Oliver, Unitarian and gay, who wrote: "There is life without love. It is not worth a bent penny..."

And I think of Amichai, who gifted us with these blessed words, shortly before he died: "Open closed open. Before we are born, everything is open without us.

For as long as we live, everything is closed within us. And when we die, everything is open again. Open closed open. That's all we are."

I open my eyes, close them and open them again, happy to be alive. I decide on eggs for breakfast, a chapel of them. And I will share them with you, if you like.

Rubbing an imaginary bent penny between my thumb and forefinger,
I realize how lucky I am—how blessed—to be in love.

Because We Are in Love

Because we are in love in Jerusalem,
I do not mind that I can see my breath,
as winter rain blows in sheets against our leaky windows.

Because we are in love in Jerusalem,
nighttime is our palette. We talk until dawn
in strokes and swirls of incandescent hues.

Because we are in love in Jerusalem,
we ignore politics, religion, the price of bread.
Everything that matters here. We, a community of two.

Because we are in love in Jerusalem,
I do not mind that the electric heater
is on your side of the bed.

The effrontery of it: to be young and in love in this venerable city.
This is a serious city. A city of blood and pain, sins and penitence.
A city with its own math (every experience squared or cubed).
The *hamsin* is more penetrating. The *tefillin* are bound tighter.
This is a city of swords, of stones, of suicide bombs.
Of political schemers, able to justify any end by any means.

But you are exquisite.
And I am no mathematician, no soldier, no penitent, no politician.

11:11. That is All.

Most mornings, at 11:11, I send you a text message that says:

11:11. That is all.

To which you respond with a text of your own:

Smiley face emoticon.

Like many rituals between husband and wife, it's hard to say how this one began. But 11:11 is more than a placeholder between 11:10 and 11:12 or the answer to the question, what's 379 + 732?

11:11 is the picket fence that surrounds our yard. It offers scant protection, with its short stature and revealing gaps; the wood, as weathered and rickety as we are. But its posts are firmly rooted and should survive for many years.

11:11 stands at attention; in respect of the sacrifices we make and that others make for us. And though there is great fortitude in these twin towers, we forget, at our peril, the unpredictable, impermanent nature of man.

11:11 saved your life. When you stood before the killing field, so afraid and called my name, it was not me (to my shame), but 11:11 that took your hand. That guided you over the trip wires to the other side.

11:11 is our four children; our joint contribution to fixing a broken world. Each of them is straight and proud, always looking up for inspiration. It's good knowing each digit is independent, yet incomplete without the others.

11:11 is the narrow bridge between reality and memory, sadness and joy, sickness and well-being, confidence and fear. 11:11 is the bridge between what we are and what we can become. And that, my love, is truly all.

Anniversary Poem

There is a fading photo of us, at 20,
on New Year's Eve in Jerusalem with
a dozen good friends, at Shemesh Grill,
where I passed on the shashlik skewers
that we ordered for the table and chose,
instead, a plate of grilled hearts, which I
knew I could not bring myself to eat, just
so that when it was placed in front of me,
I could say: "I offer you a piece of my heart."
I don't know which of our friends took the shot,
nor whether thought was given to the framing,
but the camera caught me kissing you full on the
mouth and in the background, a waiter passed
behind us carrying a tray of fresh vegetables.
When your father, who had not met me, saw
the picture, you told me he said, "nice tomatoes."
Which, whenever I think of it, makes me smile.

The Shemesh Grill is long gone. So, too, is your dad.
And I do not know where most of our Jerusalem friends
are these days.

What, after all, is one kiss in a lifetime of kisses?
But I am here with you. My heart still, always, on offer.

Why I Write Poetry

> Writing poetry is like dropping a rose petal down
> the Grand Canyon and waiting for the echo.
>
> —Don Marquis

Because one day, when I was twelve, I chose from my parent's bookshelf, *Candy is Dandy: The Best of Ogden Nash*, and read:

The ostrich roams the great Sahara.
Its mouth is wide, its neck is narra.
It has such long and lofty legs,
I'm glad it sits to lay its eggs.

And I laughed out loud.

Because a high school English teacher once told me I had a nice touch.
I dreamt of her for years.

Because a college professor, unimpressed, dismissed my poems as "pomes."
She was not the girl of my dreams.

Because I like the look of ink on a yellow pad.
When I use a red pen, the words appear to be written in blood.

Because when I need to express grief, it feels better than crying.
I still cry, too.

Because I can't hit a curve ball or build a deck.
Because I cannot give birth.

Because when I'm confused, I can strip down my thoughts.
Then, buff and polish them until they are so shiny, I can see my reflection.

Because, every now and then, I can surprise my wife with a poem.
It isn't easy to surprise someone who's known you most of your life.

I write poetry because, when I really listen, I can hear the echo.
It blows me away...it blows me away...it blows me away.

On My 50th Birthday, I Channel Ogden Nash

They say that youth is fleeting, that it's wasted on the young,
that the old are long in tooth (are the older long in tongue?).
That our time on earth is precious, it's a sin to waste a minute,
so get up off the sidelines, life's a game you should be in it.
But as the years fly by and the waist begins to spread,
and the chins begin to multiply with every slice of bread,
piled high with hot pastrami and other types of deli,
and your toes are just a memory beneath your Santa's belly,
you wonder when it happened, when began the great descent,
why you've got nothing much to show for the energy you've spent.
One day you are Adonis, the next your back is bent,
you used to have get-up-and-go, but it got up and went.
How profoundly cruel the deity, capricious and so arbitrary,
who can turn the sunny days of June into the snows of February,
one day you preen before a mirror, as if you are Greek statuary,
and next you're laid out cold and stiff, in the basement of a mortuary.
And no one's sure what happens next, though this is much discussed,
and rabbis, preachers, priests and mullahs tell us we must trust,
that the afterlife is the entire loaf, that this life's just the crust,
While ashes go to ashes and dust returns to dust.
And though such morbid thoughts are fundamentally depressing,
to know that as the years progress, you're actually regressing.
That the bloom falls off the rose, that the engine block gets cracked,
libido in repose, testosterone ransacked
(your prostate must admit, it's an accessory before the fact),
and there's no drug, no remedy, no legislative act
to halt the sharp decline of your old digestive tract.
Perhaps the only thing to do is have some herbal tea
and pray that Congress doesn't cancel Medicare Part B.

Random Walk

> A random walk is a mathematical formalization of a path that consists of a succession of random steps. For example, the search path of a foraging animal or the economic status of a gambler...
>
> —*Wikipedia*

I was out walking today and a grand piano
did not fall from the sky onto my head, nor
did the ground open up and swallow me whole!

And not once was I was struck by lighting or
bitten by a tsetse fly, both of which could
happen at any time, of course.

Most surprisingly, I did not even get eaten by
a hungry lion foraging for food, though it was
almost time for supper.

And while a gambler's good fortune as
remarkable as mine, would seem to defy the
odds, I should say that I also did not win

the lottery and was not appointed a justice
of the Supreme Court though, in the spirit
of full disclosure, had I bought a ticket

and attended law school, these negative outcomes,
perhaps, might have been avoided. But, given the
random walk of life, it is hard to say for sure.

Mind Over Matter

On a particularly turbulent flight, during which the captain announces
the attendants should take their seats (which they do with alarming speed),
I soothe my shaken psyche by repeating the unlikely words *fiery crash*

again and again in my mind, as the plane bobs and weaves through
the stormy night, like a heavyweight fighter, trained to take the
glancing blow but avoid the knockout punch that will finish him off.

I am a frequent flyer but a terrible one, my unease compounded by an
irrational, but unshakeable, precognition that my fate is to die in a fiery
crash. Or, survive one; which, oddly, seems like it could be, almost, as bad

an outcome. And, as a coping mechanism, the metronomic repetition of
the terrifying words strips them of their power over me. The words are
words no longer; they are nothing more than a series of nonsensical sounds,

almost musical, almost numinous. An overhead bin pops opens, its contents
spill to the floor and the stranger in the seat next to mine shrieks and grabs
my arm in panic. If she only knew the subversive thoughts I was thinking:

*fierycrashfierycrashfierycrashfierycrashfierycrashfierycrashfierycrashfiery
crashfierycrashfierycrashfierycraashfierycrashfierycrashfierycrashfierycrash
fierycrashfierycrashfierycrashfierycrashfierycrashfierycrashfierycrash!!!!!!!!*

I smile and assure her this will end soon. And, it will. One way or the other.
I close my eyes and the syllables fly smoothly through my mind, coasting
toward a destination unknown; where skies are clear, far beyond the horizon.

Mindfulness

My mind is like black ice.
Hidden from plain sight and dangerous to unsuspecting passers-by.

I once got fired because my mind would not tolerate fools.
One of whom was my boss.

Sometimes it seems like I've lost my mind.
Like a house key or dry-cleaning receipt that eventually turns up.

My mind keeps secrets from me.
It knows I cannot be trusted.

My mind can do 10 push-ups.
Last year it could do 20.

Given how much attention I pay to minding my Ps and Qs,
the other letters are probably getting away with murder.

Scientists say the mind's capacity decreases 15%, on average, as a person ages.
My mind is above average.

Wile E. Coyote, running off a cliff, realizes (too late),
that mind over matter is mostly a myth.

It slipped my mind to buy mangoes at the store, like you asked.
But my mind recalls the starting lineup for the '69 Cubs.

On a plane, a fellow passenger asked if I'd mind switching my aisle seat for his middle.
Why not ask for my kidney?

Ghandi said, "I will not let anyone walk through my mind with dirty feet."
Which reminds me, I've never said anything anyone would quote to make a point.

My mind has a mind of its own.
My mind wanders, but always finds the way home.

Foreign Exchange: Jerusalem '79

Just inside the Damascus Gate, in the teeming, ancient Arab souk,
mustachioed moneychangers pay the highest rates for dollars, marks,
and francs. Leading customers into cramped booths like honored guests,
they offer hand-rolled smokes and baklava, seal transactions with a loud
clap and hot mint tea in unwashed glasses. For an exchange student,
in turbulent financial times, trips to the old, walled city are necessary
to pay the bills. He rushes from booth to booth, a wad of dollars
stuffed in his pocket. First, to Hamid, then Naghib, across to Abdullah
with the crazy eyes, and back to Hamid for his final, best, black-market price.
Oh, the rush of adrenaline, the fear. Wondering, what could happen
to someone like him, in a place like this. He looks around, sees lamb
carcasses hanging from hooks, hears the crack of backgammon dice
against olivewood, the muezzin's plaintive cry. The smells, he remembers
best: grilled meats, exotic spices, sesame loaves drizzled with oil.
And other scents too: days-old garbage, rotting fruit, donkey shit
in steaming piles. All these smells mixed together, as if by an unseen
alchemist, to produce the pungent odor of commerce. He is often late
to class from these excursions and some days does not show up at all.
He sits in a café, eating hummus with warm pita, watching history unfold.
A rich exchange student. With lessons in his pocket that dollars cannot buy.

On the 150th Anniversary of the Publication, in Warsaw, of My Great-Grandfather's 13-Volume Edition of the Bible

The books bind us, though I know little about him.
Not his height or weight, not his profession.
Was he honest in his dealings? Would he drop a coin
in the beggar's cup? Did he like his wife's cooking?

All I know is he was the kind of man who shlepped
thirty pounds of books on an arduous trip. I imagine
the voyage, the heaving sea. On restless nights, he
strains to decipher the tiny text by candlelight, and

the volume he returns to, again and again, is the Book of Jonah.
Trapped in the belly of his own terrifying beast, he wonders:
Into what strange land will the Leviathan retch him out?
Without money or language, how will he feed his children?

He finds no answers. He is no scholar. He is no prophet.
His stomach will not settle and he cannot hold down food.
For you are dust and to dust shall you return.
Yes, he thinks. Books. Men. Everything.

Now, after 150 years, his books live on a shelf in my house.
They are too fragile to use but, sometimes, I remove a volume
and hold it to my face, to breathe in the musty fragrance of history.
When I turn the dusty, yellowed pages, they crumble.

What We Needed

At the exact moment on the Saturday morning mom died, had we gone
to synagogue, we might have been reciting the comforting prayer:
Blessed are You, Lord, who revives the dead.

But we chose, instead, to walk. To enjoy the warm, spring air, appreciate
the reborn trees with their nascent buds, pretending the end was not
near. And, anyhow, words of comfort were not what we needed that day.

What we needed, was for mom to rise from the hospital bed that did not
belong in her bedroom. We needed her to remove the tubes and needles
that forced air into her scarred lungs and a river of drugs into her failing system.

We needed her to brush her hair, put on pretty blouse and comfortable slacks.
And, then, we needed her to walk the few steps to her tiny kitchen, where
she'd prepared a thousand school lunches and an ocean of chicken soup.

Where she'd measured and poured, chopped and sliced, boiled and baked.
Where her daughters helped her cook epic meals that the family devoured,
like a swarm of locusts that had not eaten in seventeen years.

What we needed, that day, was for mom to make us lunch. Nothing fancy.
Maybe some pancakes with chocolate chips. How happy it would have made
her to feed us one last time. To enter paradise with a stained apron.

They say a woman of valor is hard to find; to give her credit for her labors and
let her achievements praise her at the Gates of Heaven. Blessed are You Lord,
who revives the dead; who has given us pancake batter and chocolate chips.

How I Came to Compare Visiting My Sick Uncle to Taking Fish Oil Pills

Visiting my uncle at the hospice on the day before he died,
I did not enter his room but lingered by the doorway.
He was in his final hours by then and though it would have been
nice of me to read to him or hold his hand, to send him off
wherever he was heading with the sound of a soothing voice
or warm touch, I stayed put; hoping this would end soon,
so I would not have to return.

A nurse, who had seen me visit before, stopped to chat
and praised me for "being there" for him: *"You'd be shocked
how many people don't have the heart to visit their loved ones
when it gets to this point."*

Which is kind of funny, because my uncle did not like me much,
and my heart had long since hardened against him.
But she was quite pretty, so I accepted her praise, as any hero would.
If she only knew the selfish truth: I was there for the same reason
I take fish oil pills, though they upset my stomach and give me bad breath.
They say the Omega-3 fatty acids are good for the cardiovascular system.
This may or may not be true. But why take chances, when it comes
to matters of the heart?

Having Never Written a Holocaust Poem, I Write This

I once heard, in the days before the Allies liberated
Auschwitz, there was mass confusion and the Nazis
began shooting Jews with indiscriminate fervor.
So, to save themselves, a 10-year-old girl and her
younger brother descended into a sewer beneath
the camp. To maintain sanity, the children held hands
and sang songs, remembered from their Sabbath table,
from what must have seemed like another life. Then,
as the two of them sang *"Shalom aleichem, malachei hasharet,
malachei elyon,"* other children heard the plaintive tune,
welcoming the angels from the heavenly sphere, and
descended into the sewer. And soon, they, too, were singing.
Thinking not of the heavenly spheres, not of angels.
But the notes. Only the notes. In filth to their waists,
they sang. Their voices fluid as milk, sweet as honey.
In the fetid air. Holding hands. Determined to survive.

In every generation, a Jew is commanded to feel as if
he or she experienced the exodus from Egypt.
As if he or she was present at Sinai.
I remember, once, climbing Mount Sinai with a group
of friends and proclaiming, with all the wisdom of my 19 years:
In every generation, a Jew must feel as if he or she experienced Auschwitz!
One friend pushed back: In every generation,
a Jew must feel as if he or she *never* experienced Auschwitz.
Perhaps he's right. We Jews are always climbing.
Seeking some unknown celestial summit to plant a flag in triumph.

Who, but angels, can breathe the thin air at such heights?

To Be a Jew in the Twenty-First Century

To be a Jew in the twentieth century is to be given a gift...the gift is torment
  —*Muriel Rukeyser, Letters From the Front*

Nothing has changed. The gift is still torment.
The torment of wanting. An old story by now.
A weary immigrant sets down the heavy bags
of persecution. Craves acceptance.
Trades history for the promise of a new start.
He sees a door in the distance and wants to enter.
He wants this more than he has wanted anything.
Decipherer of science, mathematics, medicine.
Surely, they will appreciate such noble contributions,
and let him in. Knowing he cannot come empty-handed,
he brings his children as an offering.

The centuries pile in an endless tower of time, eclipsing the sun.
And the Jews stand in silent horror, as an ancient darkness
descends upon the land.

On the Jewish New Year

> Let us now relate the power of this day's holiness, for it is awesome
> and frightening...On Rosh Hashanah will be inscribed...who will live,
> who will die...who by water and who by fire...who will enjoy tranquility,
> who will suffer...
>
> —U'netaneh Tokef prayer, from the Jewish New Year liturgy

One Rosh Hashanah eve, when I was ten, my friend
Mike's house was destroyed by fire. For hours
it seemed, or it might have been minutes, I watched

it burn from my bedroom window, the wild flames
illuminating the evening sky. We used to trade
baseball cards at his kitchen table and I wondered

if he was able to save them. That night, in a dream,
I stood by my window and watched Mike—South-side
Irish-Catholic—blow a shofar, tall as a ten-year-old boy.

With each blast, flames shot out, as if from the mouth
of a dragon. I knew I should watch, he was my friend.
But the light from the fire hurt my eyes and I turned away.

I have not seen Mike for forty years, do not recall his face.
Has he lived a tranquil life? Has he suffered? On Rosh
Hashanah, I remember the boys we were, sliding cards

across formica. Mantle for Maris. Killebrew for Conigliaro.
Dreaming of the cards that would, one day, bear our own faces.
Never suspecting, how awesome and frightening this life can be.

In the Age of Giants

> Methuselah lived 900 years. Methuselah lived 900 years.
> But who calls that livin' when no gal will give in,
> to no man what's 900 years?
> —*It Ain't Necessarily So (from Porgy and Bess)*

On the day that he died, Methuselah made love.
It was in his head but, nonetheless, it was glorious
to feel 300 again. How fruitful he'd been.
How he had multiplied. And, now, practically
a ghost, he felt the familiar stirring.
He had outlived everyone, but that was no blessing.
To watch a world going mad. The giants fallen.
It was hard to see the point of it all.
And, yet, there was solace in touch.
Mouth against neck. Tongue against thigh.
A perfumed hand brushed across his cheek.
Or, was it the scent of lilacs in the wind?
The tent was filled with family, their muffled cries
interrupting his dream. Sodomites. Mercenaries.
There, only, to stake their claims. And, in a corner,
his grandson, Noah; his favorite. Building some
crazy boat—obsessed with animals—but a good boy.
Maybe there's hope for the world, after all.
And, then, Methuselah shut his eyes and resumed
his lovemaking; crying out his lover's name
with one final, giant breath.

A Man Shall Not Lie

> A man shall not lie with a man, as one lies with a woman;
> it is abomination.
>
> —*Leviticus 18:22*

When he was 18, my good friend went to his rabbi
to confess, as if he was a criminal. Which, in a community
like ours—where the words of the Torah dictate the details
of our lives, from great to minute—perhaps he was.
The rabbi, by all reports, was respectful. He listened
without interrupting. He had counseled many boys
like this one and knew he could fix him.

God tests us all, he said, stroking his beard, and our job
is to banish the evil inclination. So, he told my friend
to wear a thick rubber band around his wrist and snap it
every time he felt an abominable urge. Instead of laughing
at the absurd notion or walking out in dignified protest,
my friend acquiesced; grateful, no doubt, to be given
a path to redemption.

Many years later, my own rabbi gives a sermon about
gay marriage, excoriating the "tsunami of immorality" that,
he insists, threatens to drown us all. It is our Torah obligation
to fight back, he says. This is what God expects of us, he says.
I have never heard him speak with such passion, such purpose.
He is so sure of himself. It is frightening how sure of himself.

And, as he pontificates the tired talking points of the
Modern-Orthodox rabbinate—*we must love the sinner,
my friends, but hate the sin*—I think of you. Of the sadness
you must have endured, the loneliness. I remember we talked
about girls, the way teenage boys do. How did I not know
you were different? How could I not see you, drowning
in the tsunami of my ignorance?

Oh, the things we do and do not do, in the name of God.

Fathers and Sons

> And Avraham stretched forth his hand and took the knife to slay his son.
> —*Genesis* 22:10

The midrash teaches that when Avraham pressed the knife
against Yitzchak's neck, just before the moment of sacrifice,
both cried tears of joy, privileged to obey the divine decree.

The angels—hovering, horrified—watch this scene
and cannot hold back their own tears, which fall like rain.
The angels know it is not their place—they exist to serve—

but plead with God, saying the words Avraham will not:
*"Didn't You promise descendants, numerous as the stars?
As the sand on the shore? Call this off, we beg you Lord!"*

At that, God is sufficiently moved and commands one
of them to call out *"Avraham, Avraham,"* and it is over.
But a father knows it is never over.

We bring our boys into the world, spilling love onto them like
some holy, anointing oil. They are new and improved versions
of us, or so we hope. We try to recreate ourselves in these

unsuspecting creatures, who want to believe that their fathers
are gods. And though we love our sons more than our precious
selves, sometimes a father is powerless.

Sometimes, sons are in the wrong place at the wrong time,
sometimes they get sick. Sometimes sons are lost in battle .
And, sometimes, they are simply lost.

Fathers, sons themselves, know the unsettling truth.
Life and knife are one. And God, at his whetstone, watches;
the tears of angels deep, by now, as rivers, seas, oceans.

On the Day His Father Died, Esau Wept

Can you recall a time, and a place, when you were happy?
A time before the brute force with which you attack every problem
made you hard. A time before the weight of expectations became
too heavy to bear. Was there ever a moment?

You try to ignore the demons that whisper to you; their obsequious
compliments, their evil exhortations: "You are strong, like the bear.
Swift as a colt. You owe nothing to anyone. Will you allow him
to steal your birthright? Your hate is wholly justified. Your hate is holy."

But you see their point. This is who you are, how you were created.
Before your lungs filled with air for the first time, you felt the urge
to acquire, to dominate. So eager to enter the world, you showed
your brother your foot. And, so, the course of your life was set.

And Jacob, who could not shoot a straight arrow, is also who he
was created to be. No innocent, but the plotting predator, waiting
to pick off his prey in a moment of weakness. You've so much
in common. It's just that he's better at it than you.

And, yet, the wounds you've suffered today—duplicitous brother,
devious mother—are too much, even for you. Your voice breaking,
you cry out, "Father, haven't you a blessing for me?" And the demons,
unsettled by emotion, are mute. Alone. You've always been alone.

Dinah Took a Walk One Lovely Day

> And Dinah...went out to see the daughters of the land.
> And Shechem...the prince of the land, saw her; and he took her,
> and lay with her, and violated her.
>
> —*Genesis 34:1-2*

Dinah took a walk one lovely day.
But darkness soon eclipsed the warming sun.
To some men, women are no more than prey.

He saw a piece of meat, a fresh filet.
And snatched her from the road, that's how it's done.
Dinah took a walk one lovely day.

Who knows if she screamed NO!, she had no say.
He would not stop until the deed was done.
To some men, women are no more than prey.

And who was she, a girl, to disobey?
If only she'd been one of Jacob's sons.
Dinah took a walk one lovely day.

Her deepest fear was they'd cast her away.
Damaged goods, no good to anyone.
To some men, women are no more than prey.

The price of evil fell on her to pay.
Where was God? Maybe there is none.
Dinah took a walk one lovely day.
To some men, women are no more than prey.

The Four Species

> And you shall take...the fruit of splendid trees (etrog), branches of palm trees (lulav) and boughs of leafy trees (hadas) and willows of the brook (aravah), and you shall rejoice before the LORD your God for seven days.
>
> —*Leviticus 23:40 (Torah portion for the first day of Sukkoth)*

It is said that the *lulav*, which tastes good but has no smell, symbolizes those who study Torah, but do not possess good deeds. The *hadas*, with no taste, but satisfying smell, symbolizes those who possess good deeds, but do not study Torah. The *aravah* has neither taste nor smell, symbolizing those who lack both Torah and good deeds. The *etrog* has both a good taste and good smell, symbolizing those who have both Torah and good deeds. In binding together the *lulav, hadas* and *aravah* and holding them next to the tasty, fragrant *etrog*, we celebrate the unity of the Jewish people.

Sukkoth: Holiday of the senses. And grand delusions.

Because

> Do not boil a kid, in her mother's milk
>
> —Exodus 23:19

Because God created the world and saw it was good…
Because He created Adam and Eve as helpmates…
Because God destroyed the world but had Noah build an ark…
Because God let the waters retract and a dove plucked an olive branch…
Because Avram went forth from the land of his birth…
Because God changed his name to Avraham…
Because God promised Avraham children as numerous as the stars…
Because Sarah laughed…
Because an angel said, "Avraham, Avraham," and Yitzchak was saved…
Because Avraham paid for Sarah's gravesite, to be clear about who owns that land…
Because Yaakov worked an extra seven years to marry Rachel…
Because he knew how to wrestle with angels…
Because he knew how to cook a mouth-watering stew…
Because Rachel weeps for her children and will not be comforted…
Because Yosef was a show-off and a dandy and a dreamer…
Because he did not succumb to desire…
Because he exacted revenge on his brothers but, in the end, forgave them…
Because he wept when his father died and returned his bones to Canaan…
Because a new Pharaoh rose, who did not know Yosef…
Because two midwives saved Jewish babies from a monstrous decree…
Because baby Moses survived a perilous cruise down the Nile…
Because the burning bush did not consume itself…
Because God commanded Moses to lead the Jews to freedom…
Because God hardened Pharaoh's heart…
Because there were frogs here, frogs there, frogs hopping everywhere…
Because God split the sea and finished off Pharaoh…
Because He brought the Jews to a mountain, raised it above their heads like a barrel and said, If you accept these commandments, fine; if not then here your grave shall be…
And because the people replied in unison, We will do *and* we will listen.…

Because of it all, when I accidentally use a spoon from the meat drawer
to eat a scoop of Ben & Jerry's, somewhere, a baby goat sucking at
her mother's teats stops for a moment and bleats. The sound travels
to the Kingdom of Heaven, where one of God's angels takes out a red pen
and, scowling, enters a mark in my permanent record.

Upon Unexpectedly Finding
a Long-Forgotten Keepsake

While looking for something else in an old box of files, I found a poem, handwritten on four lined sheets, by an old friend from college, also a David. Titled Jerusalem, the poem is naive, angry, rude, funny, wise.

Only the young write like this; each line to the margins. As if the page-edge is all that keeps the words from shooting into space, like heat-seeking missiles.

How have I not thought of him in thirty years? We both loved Ginsberg and read *Howl*, out loud, on a bus ride to Ein Gedi; the Hebrew speakers looking up when, uninhibited, he stood, confident and handsome, and recited the famous first line by memory:

I saw the best minds of my generation destroyed by madness,
starving hysterical naked, dragging themselves through
the negro streets at dawn, looking for an angry fix.

He was a fine poet, better than me. We agreed that a great poem is one you are jealous you could not write yourself. Once, we both liked a beauty from Brooklyn named Raizy. He said, I'm going to marry that girl! and I backed off. But I didn't mind. I liked him better than I liked her.

I have his poem, because one night he asked for my honest opinion. "I know it's good," he said. "But does it make you jealous?" I took the four pages, jealous already.

Jerusalem, February seventh or eighth of my youth...I exist now
and you take advantage...I search the wrong cities, they are all you...
I knocked on your front door yesterday, but no one answered...
I left a note. Did you receive it?... Do not whore your beauty with
hotel splendor...can you not admire the gnarled majesty of olive trees?
Jerusalem, if I pay will you listen?...Jerusalem, state your price...

David, my long-lost friend. Are you still confident and handsome? Did you marry Raizy, as you pledged? Have you made peace with Jerusalem? Has she answered your plaintive pleas?

David, after thirty years, do you still write your fine poems?

Advice to My Children
About Handling Criticism

Give anyone a hammer, they can tear down a house. And how satisfying
it feels, to some, to punch through drywall, rip out pipe, shatter a chandelier
to watch the shards fly in every direction.

And if you gave such a person a jerry-can of gas and book of matches,
he or she would be unable to resist setting the house ablaze; the heat of
their anger a thousand times more combustible than any man-made structure.

It is not within such people to appreciate that, once, a foundation was carefully
measured and poured. Drapes were chosen to complement the rug in the hall.
That each night, in the kitchen, someone prepared a meal and a family was fed.

You will meet people like this. And, because you're not like them, because
you've never tasted the bitter waters with which they brew their coffee and
brush their teeth, their words will hurt you like bee stings or bed bugs

burrowing beneath your skin. But, their power over you is an illusion, the
cheapest parlor trick, waiting to be exposed. So, children, here is my advice:
Look such people in their eyes, though they will desperately try to look away.
And, then, think of a kitchen table filled with food. A happy family being fed.

Upon Seeing My Children's Newly Built School for the First Time

For the founders and builders of The Chicagoland Jewish High School

We are dreamers of outlandish dreams,
diggers of holes, movers of earth.
Sinking pillars into bedrock, we aspire
to permanence in an impermanent world
and though, in time, all man-made things
crumble, the outlandish dream survives.
For we will bring the inanimate to life,
fill empty rooms with words and song,
splash walls with color, open windows
to let in the sweet, invigorating breeze.
We do this not for fame, not for fortune,
not even to leave behind our names.
We do this because it is what we can do;
to fill the void, to articulate the grand vision,
to create, as we were created.

Oh, to dream outlandish dreams!

How Deeply Rooted is the Tree of Life

When my wife and I were young, we attended a small synagogue
with our two-year-old, Jessica, who'd toddle back and forth
through the cotton sheet separating the men and women,
spending a few minutes with my wife, a few minutes with me.

Back and forth, back and forth. A toddler metronome.
Back and forth, back and forth. As if she owned the joint.

And as the Torah scroll was returned to the ark, I'd pick her up
and press my stubbled, Sabbath cheek against the softness of her's
and sing the poetic words from Proverbs:

The Torah is a tree of life for those who grasp onto it.

Once, Jessie started singing with me, and the congregants,
caught off guard by the sweet sound, laughed.
But she kept on singing, getting all the words right
(it must have been the first song she knew by heart).

And that was the exact moment, I learned the meaning of life:

Hold on to Torah. And hold on to the people you love.

My Son-in-Law, the Rabbi, is a Clown

This sounds awful, I know. As if I am one of those dads who thinks no one is good enough for my daughter. Or, as if I have something against rabbis, or clowns, or both. Not so: I simply wanted to write a poem called *My Son-in-Law, the Rabbi, is a Clown*, because the title made me laugh out loud. And I knew it would make Adam, my son-in-law, laugh out loud too.

Ask Adam, the rabbi, a question about Jewish law and he will answer it, according to his training. And if you are a child, sick in a hospital bed, he will try to make you laugh, by tripping over his clown-sized-22-sneakers, by crashing together a pair of cymbals, by telling a dumb knock-knock joke, also as he has been trained.

Neither of these jobs are easy and I do not know which matters more. When a Jew asks a rabbi a question about Jewish law, the answer can dictate a lifetime of observance. But when a medical clown sneezes snot-scarves from a red, rubber nose onto a 7-year-old with no eyebrows, the child's giggles cannot be contained.

They seek the ether through open doors and vents in the wall, they leave the room attached to the coattails of doctors as they make their rounds. A sick child's laughter floats above tall rooftops, through clouds and space, past stars and galaxies, straight into paradise itself. And there, Aaron and Moses, Hillel and Shamai, Rambam and Ramban, the Ba'al Shem and Chofetz Chaim

and all the great rabbis of every generation reside in God's presence. Surprisingly, they do not discuss Torah, as might be expected. There are no heavy Talmudic volumes floating on desks of clouds, no spirited debates. And no one asks God the terrible, impertinent question with which we struggle here on earth: *Why do the innocent suffer?*

Instead, a procession of bearded old men, some in biblical robes, some in long, black coats, line up before a tiny automobile, wondering how many rabbis can fit into a sedan.

Upon Meeting my Granddaughter for the First Time

For Charlie Ruby

You lay sleeping, on my chest, like your mother used to.
Three days old and growing on me already. Your body
seems heavier than 7-pounds, 6-ounces and, soon, your
warmth and the rhythm of your breath have lulled me to
a dream. I see you at 6, reciting the four questions. At 12,
chanting from the Torah. Now, you are graduating from college.
Now, you stand under the chuppah. Now, you are a mother yourself.
And, somehow, I know you are a new kind of Jewish woman.
Defined not by the value of rubies, not by your husband's praise.
No man controls you. No rabbi dictates what you may study,
where you may pray. In Jerusalem, you sing the Hallel and
the black hats cover their ears. But your voice is a whirlwind,
an earthquake. The pent-up force of a thousand generations
of silenced women. It carries through streets and neighborhoods,
study halls and synagogues. Impossible to ignore. Impossible
to stifle. It penetrates the heart. It penetrates the soul.
It penetrates, even, the ancient stones. And, then, a familiar
odor wakes me from my reverie. You are no prophet, darling.
No crusader. Just a baby, whose diaper is full. Let's get that
taken care of little Charlie. Little love. Little girl of my dreams.

What Jessica Hears

My daughter was born on the first day of Rosh Hashanah.
And on that day, instead of hearing the 100 blasts of the shofar
in my synagogue, I listened to Jessica's cries (at least 100 of them),
with the other members of her first congregation: a minyan
of doctors, nurses and orderlies; her mother leading
the service in an elegant hospital gown.

It is taught that the notes of the shofar— the single, uninterrupted *t'kiah*,
the wavering calls of *shvarim*, and the staccato sobs of *t'ruah*—
describe the condition of the soul during a lifetime.
We are born clear and straight, succumb to crookedness as adults,
and grieve for our mortality in old age. But the final blast of the shofar,
the breathtaking *t'kiah g'dolah*—an extended *t'kiah*, powerful and pure—
reminds us that God receives the penitent, who seeks to return
to a state of innocence.

Walking to synagogue on Rosh Hashanah, when Jessica was 10,
she told me the shofar sounds like a starving child.
Where she got this, I do not know, my daughter, who has never gone
to bed hungry. But that day, I prayed for all the world's starving children.
And for Jessie, her soul still *t'kiahlike*.

And, as the sound of the shofar filled the room, I could not stop thinking of her.
Holding back tears, I listened, so as not to miss a single note. I listened,
trying to remember what it's like to be 10. I listened, for the sound that I used to know,
but have not heard for a very long time: the sweet, uncomplicated voice of God.

Matt Turns Six

Little man. Gap-toothed, milk-mustachioed dervish,
turning chocolate-colored in the summer sun.

New rules at six. No public displays of affection.
Lots of Legos. Long games of catch. And, girls stink.

The day you were born, I cried. Because God created
a world in which parents cannot protect their children.

Now, you say, Abba, I'm six. Take the training wheels off my bike!
You don't know that you'll fall, though you'll learn soon enough.

So, I'll run behind you. I'll pick you up and hold you close.
I'll feel your tears on my face, your racing heart against my own.

Moments like these are a precious gift.
Bury your head in my chest, little man. No one but God is watching.

What Matters

When you were point guard on your high school
team (a leader, even as a boy), you looked to me
for advice. Every game, at halftime, you'd find me
just before the whistle blew and I would tell you,
the guy you are guarding has a weak left hand, or
take the open jump-shot instead of passing the ball
inside. It did not matter that, in the locker room,
your coach had already told you the same thing (or
the exact opposite). It did not matter who saw us, or
that your teammates might have thought it odd to
see you with me as they formed their layup lines.
All that mattered, was my hand cupped around
your neck, your head tilted slightly forward, so as
not to miss a single, whispered word. In that moment,
in that connection, you understood. No one cared more
and no one cared less, about how you played, than I.

The Pain That Cuts Deep

> A youth and a lass slowly march toward the nation...dressed in battle gear...
> full of endless fatigue, yet the dew of youth is still seen on their head...Then a
> nation in tears and amazement will ask: "who are you?" And they will answer
> quietly, "We are the silver platter on which the Jewish nation was given."
>
> —Natan Alterman, *The Silver Platter*

When my son was 13, with a sweet jump shot but 4 inches too short
to make the team, he wailed on the car ride home, his grief real and deep.
And though I understood why he had been cut (in more ways than one),
I had to pull over, unable to see the road through my own sodden eyes.
But I knew what he didn't; he'd never be cut from a team again.

When my son was 16, he told me and my wife that he needed
to go to Poland, to see the camps. Said he would pay the $2,000
himself. We asked him why and he answered with his own question:
"How can I pass up the privilege of being a witness?" And, as if
we needed more convincing: "That generation is almost gone.
They are relying on the witnesses to tell their stories."

When my son was 18, he told me and my wife he was joining
the Israeli army. We asked him why and he answered, again,
with a question: "How can I pass up the privilege to serve
in the first Jewish army since Bar Kokhba?"

Afraid, knowing the now well-built point guard, with a killer jump-shot
would not be sitting at a desk, I said, in a voice too harsh: "This isn't a novel.
You're not Ari Ben Canaan." Instead of responding in kind, and
with a literary reference better than mine, he disarmed me with a smile.
"The Jewish nation," he said, "wasn't given on a silver platter."

When he was 24, my son, the lieutenant, came home on furlough.
He does not discuss his life as a soldier and this is probably for the best.
And he has never spoken to us about the camps. But that's okay.
When he is called, the witness will take the stand.

Throughout the too-short visit, just to look at him leads me to tears,
but I make no effort to conceal my sodden eyes. Matt learned, long ago,
to appreciate the pain that cuts deep. And though he is now, forever,

beyond the dew of youth, I do not have to ask him who he is.
He is the silver platter on which my life was given.

A Soldier Learns to Sleep

wherever and whenever he can. Once,
he slept in the back of a truck, heading
to battle on the Syrian border. Undisturbed
by the rutted road or sound of gunfire
in the distance, he dreamed he was
in bed with his wife, their infant son
nestled between them. When the truck
stopped, they had to poke his shoulder
with the butt of an M-16 to wake him.

That day, Tal, Yoav, and Itamar fell.

Years later, in bed with his wife, he
dreams he is riding in the back of a truck,
heading to battle on the Syrian border.
Next to him is his son. Undisturbed by
the rutted road or sound of gunfire in the
distance, his son sleeps, like a soldier.

Reality, memory, dream, nightmare.
When the conscious and unconscious
converge, even the dead awaken.

A Little Bit Good, A Little Bit Not So Good

For Rebecca, whose sandal broke, on a hot afternoon in Jerusalem

Rebecca, age six, is trying on sandals—every sandal, it seems—
in a cramped shoe-store on Jaffa Road. At first, I think she can't
make up her mind, amidst the strange surroundings.
But this doesn't seem right. She is too calm, too patient,
condescending, even, to me and my wife. And to the scowling salesman,
an old man in black shoes, who grunts each time he has to fetch her
a different size or color, only to hear the cryptic words she declares
when we ask: What about this pair?

A little bit good, a little bit not so good.

In the outdoor market, just outside, the mid-day din rises.
A jackhammer pulverizes Jerusalem stone.
Fishmongers bellow, fruit-sellers shout, falafel balls fry.
A street musician strums his guitar, singing a song
by Bob Dylan, badly.
An Egged bus stops, brakes screeching.
A driver honks his horn, another honks back,
and then everyone is honking, honking in harmony.
Some honk long, some honk in staccato bursts,
like a symphony of shofar-blowers,
supplicating to the God of Gridlock, as if to say:

Don't even think about ignoring me.
I have important things to do and places to go.

But our Rebecca has no place to go. And nothing more important to do,
than choose the exact, right, perfect pair of sandals.

How wonderful it is to be six years old.
How wonderful it is to buy a new pair of shoes.
How wonderful it is to be in Jerusalem, on a hot afternoon on Jaffa Road.

Leaving Home

Before you left, you gave me a gift: a framed
picture you took of your bike. A heavy Schwinn
without gears or handbrakes, its bright green frame

juxtaposed against the brilliant, blue palette of Lake
Michigan on a sunny, summer day. With your steady
hands and artist's eyes, you positioned the Schwinn

in such a way it looks like you could hop on and,
with a few thrusts of your cross-country-hardened legs,
catapult onto the surface of the great lake.

I imagine you taking off, picking up speed as you pass
incredulous swimmers, spraying them with your wake.
Ignoring the angry lifeguard's bullhorned cry:

Come back to shore IMMEDIATELY! His thin voice
recedes as, unafraid, you head past the breaker into
open water. You spin the pedals easily, skimming waves

and vaulting swells, as if you and the Schwinn are
weightless. Suddenly, inspired, you pull back on the
handlebars and are airborne. You are breaking laws

of nature, but never have you felt more connected to
the natural world. From up high, you see for miles in
every direction, as a bird might (or an angel), and you

are no longer pedaling. The jet stream propels you
and you are drawn higher and higher towards the
beautiful, beckoning sun. You've flown in an airplane

many times, enclosed and harnessed, prisoner to the
technology of how to get from Point A to B, but this
is different. This dazzling, magical flight isn't about

reaching a destination, but how to get there. It's about
freedom and creativity, enlightenment and wonder.
And if God's presence is sometimes difficult for you

to feel with your feet on the ground, up here you appreciate
the vast order that exists within chaos. For the first time,
you understand that beyond the horizon is more horizon.

And beyond the galaxy are more galaxies. Yet, somehow,
this doesn't scare you. It only makes you wonder how far
you can travel while the ride lasts.

Once, when you were little, a house came up for sale down
the block and you asked us to buy it so, when you grew up,
you could stay close to me and mom forever.

Now, someone else lives in that house we did not buy for you.
And your bright green Schwinn is parked in the garage,
where you left it, waiting for its rider and a sunny, summer day.

When you come back to earth, I know you will find your way home.

"My Name Is Rebecca…But Most People Call Me Reby"

This is how you present yourself to the world. But if it
was up to me, whenever you meet someone new, you
would say: "My name is Rebecca, but my abba calls me
Rebecca-Bunny. Or, sometimes, Bunster, for short.
And he often uses my Hebrew names in various forms:
Rivka, Rivkaleh and Rivka Malka—Rivka the Queen.
Occasionally, he greets me with a *Reeee-Becca*,
drawing out the "e" and emphasizing the "b" because
he likes the way it sounds. And, from time to time, I am
even Rivka-Bivka, a name he concocted when I was a baby
and he would pace with me, in his arms late at night,
hypnotizing us both to sleep with those four silly syllables:
Rivka-Bivka, Rivka-Bivka, Rivka-Bivka."

And now you look for your first job and I suppose this might
be a bit much information to include in a cover letter or begin
an interview. And, of course, it is not up to me. Like most things,
I am finding. So, Reby, go forth into the world and make a name
for yourself. It's okay. I know who you are.

You are my sweetie-pie. My dolly. My love. My life.

Watching a Football Game Before Dawn With My 10-Year-Old Son

At 3:30, I wake Joshua and turn on the TV in our
small hotel room, just outside the Ramon Crater.
We have traveled thousands of miles to see this hole,
the product of 300-million years of inexorable forces.

In a few hours we will be deep inside, beneath the
shadows of limestone walls, looking for fresh dung,
hoping to see an ibex climbing the sheer cliffs;
to snap its picture; to capture a moment of grace.

But now, a satellite dish, defying the remoteness
of this place and with no respect for time zones
or circadian rhythms, beams the Chicago Bears and
Atlanta Falcons onto the small television screen.

Joshua climbs into bed with me, his bare feet cold.
I should say a prayer. I should thank God for
bringing me to this moment, for this world of wonders:
for the crater, for the ibex, for satellite television.

But my son's toes are cold and the game is starting.
Perhaps, I will pray later. Perhaps, I will write a poem.

Shooting Hoops Before Dawn
With My 16-Year-Old Son

Each morning I rebound shot after shot, and quickly return the ball
to his impatient hands. He is afraid to slow down, lose his rhythm;
as if each shot is connected to prior shots and every shot to come.
Four hundred guided missiles, in less than an hour.

He is the careful warrior covering his tracks. The archeologist, searching
for something shiny just beneath the surface. The student of history, who
knows that those who fail to learn from the past, are doomed to hit less
than nine of ten free-throws from the charity stripe.

About halfway through his workout, as the sun rises, it shines through
the windows high above the court and hits him like bright lights on a
Broadway stage. At this hour, no one else is here to see his performance,
how he cuts left or right with equal ease, how perfect his body language.

And yet, he does love a crowd. To see the bleachers filled with people
who have known him his entire life. To hear his name announced
with the starting five. To know that a particular girl is watching him.
To know what it feels like to have someone watch you, like that.

But, at 6:00 AM, an audience would be superfluous and, anyhow, there is much
work to do before show time. He is content to rehearse his part. A monologue
of crossovers, jumpers, and lefty lay-ups. Chasing a rare miss, hardwood squeaking
beneath my heavy feet, Joshua smiles at me as I pass him the ball.

When he is ready, when the stands are empty, and he takes off his uniform
for the last time, I will pass other things to him. That has always been
my job. But, not today. How glad I am, for mornings like this. Glad to still be
of use. How grateful I am for the ball and hoop and the glorious games of life.

Upon Speaking to My Son's High School Basketball Team Before What Turns Out to be Their Final Game

For Joshua, Jeremy, Avidan, Hillel and Nathaniel

If we lose tonight, the season is over. But, if we win,
the season will still be over, one week from now.
So, too, your high school careers.

But this is the nature of life. All things good, come to an end.
All things bad, too, by the way. And hard as finishing this
fantastic journey may be for you, it's harder for us.

We watched you fall in love with the game. Took you to the
JCC on Sunday mornings, instead of sleeping in. Planted hoops
in our driveways. Bought you extravagant sneakers.

We drove hours in snowstorms, to hear the hardwood squeak
and drum of balls. We struggled to say the correct thing when
you lost and when you cried, we cried with you.

But we also reveled in your victories. Raising our arms to the sky.
Forgetting our failures for a few hours. Losing our voices, cheering:
Go Tigers! Go Tigers! Go Tigers!

And, now an admission: we stole from you, without shame or
remorse. We stood at the edge of the court and secretly snatched
a bit of the energy you threw off every time you streaked by.

We did it because we didn't think you would miss it. We did it
because it felt so good. Like the first real day of spring, when you
throw your coat to the ground and raise your face to the sun.

We did it because you are young and we are no longer, and we needed it
in ways you will not understand for many years. Until you have sons
and daughters of your own, streaking past you on the majestic court.

I hope you win tonight. But whatever happens, I hope you'll remember
how beautiful it was. I hope you'll remember this marvelous moment
in the history of your lives.

I hope, years from now, when each of you consider the trajectory of your life, you can summon the vision of an eternal boy and recognize that like basketball, life is a game of exquisite beauty and infinite rewards.

Ode to Our High School Gym

For Jeff

Here, we danced to the beat of the hardwood squeak,
How many hours did we spend, shooting jump shots,
practicing our crossover dribbles, playing H-O-R-S-E?
This was the place we were most at ease in the world.
A sanctuary from fears and doubts, from troubles at home,
from the pain of an unrequited love. No less a classroom
than the others in the building, we slogged through math
and science and bible and Talmud, barely conscious,
because when school let out, we were rewarded with
the ball and the hoop. Drowning in a high tide of hormones
this was the place we pushed ourselves to grow strong and swift;
glorious in our hard, healthy bodies, glorious in our youth.
Here, we learned nothing worthwhile is given.
Here, we learned sacrifice assures nothing.
This was the place we discovered victory isn't as rewarding
as you think it will be, nor is loss as shattering.
This was the sacred place where cheerleaders,
in skimpy skirts, called out our names,
as if we were immortals:

"Jeffrey, Jeffrey, he's our man! If he can't do it, David can!"

Boys Fool Themselves That They Can Fly

In my dream I hear the drum of balls,
And am transported back across the years.
So simple then, were my life's protocols,
And in the dream a memory reappears.

We sprint, we shoot, we run our drills,
Our sweat drips to the floor.
Hoping that the work instills
The strength to fly, to soar.

A teammate passes the leather sphere,
I squeeze its pebbled grain to get a grip,
And all distractions round me disappear,
Amidst the humble joy of fellowship.

Boys fool themselves that they can fly.
Men know the truth and all such truth implies.

Trader's Lament

How much he makes defines his self-esteem,
And every day his wealth appreciates,
But when he sleeps, what does the trader dream?

A war, a drought, unseemly as they seem,
Are nothing more than unfortunate fates,
How much he makes defines his self-esteem.

Does he hear the frightened child's scream,
See the withered fields desiccate?
When he sleeps, what does the trader dream?

It's not as if his goal is to blaspheme,
He hopes this is enough to exculpate,
How much he makes defines his self-esteem.

What good is guilt? Guilt cannot redeem.
Although he fears that reckoning awaits,
When he sleeps, what does the trader dream?

His sadness is an ever-present theme,
A grief he cannot quite articulate,
How much he makes defines his self-esteem,
When he sleeps, what does the trader dream?

As All Martyrs, Should Be Remembered

> Leave behind your sorrows/Let this day be the last
> Tomorrow there'll be sunshine/And all this darkness past
> Big wheels roll through fields/Where sunlight streams
> Meet me in the land of hopes and dreams.
>
> —*Bruce Springsteen*

On the day Oscar Alberto Martinez and his 23-month-old daughter Angie Valeria drowned in the Rio Grande, I'm flying over states that helped elect a tyrant. Seeking solace in poetry, in music, I scroll through my phone's playlists and the choice is easy. Who better than The Boss, to elevate my spirit? To remind me that today may be awful but tomorrow will be better?

But what solace are poetry and music, against the image of Valeria's tiny arm slung across the back of her father's neck? What comfort can there be, when fat fingers tweet hateful words throughout the hours when sane people sleep? From where will relief come, when the richest country in the history of the world, shuns the weak, the deprived, the frightened?

Soon, I'll arrive in Silicon Valley, free and fortunate to pursue my own hopes and dreams. Feeling guilty for my privilege, I understand that the solace I seek can only be found in action. So, I will raise my voice in protest. I'll send money to those in need. And, soon, I will vote to remove the tyrant and his enablers from office.

But, above all, I will remember their names:

Oscar Alberto Martinez.
Angie Valeria Martinez.

As all martyrs, should be remembered.

Miracles

> Just as it may be said that for the heretic there are no answers, so may it be
> said that for the skeptic there are no miracles...
>
> —*Rabbi Shlomo Riskin*

A friend, a non-believer, asks me why God no longer
performs flashy miracles, as he did in biblical times.

*Has He lost his touch? If God exists, let Him show
Himself to me in a burning bush that does not consume itself!*

What can I say? He is an old friend and I am used
to his derision, when it comes to matters of faith.

And though I believe, with complete faith, that God
appeared to Moses in that burning bush, I do not tell

my friend he is missing the point. The burning bush
is no more miraculous than the bush itself.

And the fire that burns but does not consume,
smolders deep within, even, the skeptic.

Acknowledgements

I extend my thanks to Ami Kaye, Publisher and Managing Editor of Glass Lyre Press, who invited me to write this book based on hearing me read *And God Created Hummus* at an open mic event. Her kindness, encouragement, and patience are much appreciated, particularly given the multiple deadlines I missed. Also, thanks to Steve Asmussen and Linda Kim at GLP for their help with the layout and editing.

Thanks and love to my children, their spouses and significant others and my three grandchildren, all of whom provide me with endless inspiration. And, a special thanks to my sweet Rebecca, who dropped everything she was doing to help her helpless abba create a cover for this book.

Finally, thanks to my wife Lauren. Most of the poems in this book are about you Laur. In fact, pretty much everything I write is to get your attention. So I'll shut up for a change and let another poet—one of our favorites—speak for me:

> *It was such an era*
> *that happiness came through anger,*
> *we laughed about everything,*
> *we burnt whatever went in our hands,*
> *there was nothing left*
> *but to embrace the trouble,*
> *to say*
> *"yesterday was good*
> *and so it will be tomorrow too."*
>
> —Shlomo Artzi

That is all.

Glass Lyre Press

exceptional works to replenish the spirit

Glass Lyre Press is an independent literary publisher interested in technically accomplished, stylistically distinct, and original work. Glass Lyre seeks diverse writers that possess a dynamic aesthetic and an ability to emotionally and intellectually engage a wide audience of readers.

Glass Lyre's vision is to connect the world through language and art. We hope to expand the scope of poetry and short fiction for the general reader through exceptionally well-written books, which evoke emotion, provide insight, and resonate with the human spirit.

Poetry Collections
Poetry Chapbooks
Select Short & Flash Fiction
Anthologies

www.GlassLyrePress.com

www.ingramcontent.com/pod-product-compliance
Lightning Source LLC
Chambersburg PA
CBHW030348100526
44592CB00010B/878